Violin Concerto
in G minor

BWV 1056R

By

Johann Sebastian Bach

A Score for Violin and Piano

1738

British Library Cataloguing-in-Publication Data
A catalogue record for this book is available from
the British Library

CONCERTO.

J. S. Bach.

8980   Copyright 1949 by C. F. Peters Corporation, New York

* If "ossia" is used, the piano plays:
* Falls "ossia" benutzt wird, spielt der Begleiter:

8

Cb.u.Vcell.

8980